MANAGING STRESS FOR MENTAL FITNESS

Revised Edition

Merrill F. Raber, MSW, Ph.D.
and
George Dyck, M.D.

A FIFTY MINUTE™ SERIES BOOK

CRISP PUBLICATIONS, INC.
Menlo Park, California

MANAGING STRESS FOR MENTAL FITNESS

Revised Edition
(Previously Published as Mental Fitness)

Merrill F. Raber, MSW, Ph.D. and George Dyck, M.D.

CREDITS
Editor: **Michael G. Crisp**
Layout and Composition: **Interface Studio**
Cover Design: **Carol Harris**
Artwork: **Ralph Mapson**

Copyright © 1987, 1993 by Crisp Publications, Inc.
Printed in the United States of America

Distribution to the U.S. Trade:

National Book Network, Inc.
4720 Boston Way
Lanham, MD 20706
1-800-462-6420

Library of Congress Catalog Card Number 92-074205
Raber, Merrill F. and Dyck, George
Managing Stress For Mental Fitness (Revised)
Previously published as Mental Fitness
ISBN 1-56052-200-3

This book is printed on recyclable paper with soy ink.

PREFACE

During the past decade considerable attention has been devoted to the importance of good physical health. The result has been impressive. Large numbers of people now exercise regularly, watch their diets and take other preventative health measures.

This book was developed to focus similar attention on the topic of managing stress to maintain good mental health. Many of the principles presented in this brief book can be developed and practiced like a thoughtful exercise program or diet.

The pressures of life are many. It is important to remember that everyone experiences some stress. Stress is normal and, properly managed, can be useful. This book will focus on finding the level of stress that may be useful for you, and teach you ways to recognize and avoid stress beyond that level. Other topics will help you understand the basic ingredients of good mental health, improve self-awareness and self-image, and clarify the link between physical wellness and emotional wellness.

One reading will simply point you in the right direction. Completing the various exercises and activities can be a significant step toward self-awareness and growth in the challenging arena of your emotional health.

Good luck!

       Merrill F. Raber, MSW, Ph.D.   George Dyck, M.D.

CONTRACT*

I, _____ , hereby agree to

(Your name)

meet with the individual designated below within thirty days

to discuss my progress toward incorporating the basic

ingredients for managing stress and good mental health

presented in this program. The purpose of this session will be

to *review* areas of strength and establish action steps for areas

where improvement may still be required.

_____

Signature

I agree to meet with the above individual on

_____

Month   *Date*   *Time*

at the following location.

_____

_____

Signature

* This agreement can be initiated by either you or anyone
  whose judgment you respect. Its purpose is to motivate you
  to incorporate important mental health principles into your
  daily activities.

ABOUT THIS BOOK

Managing Stress for Mental Fitness is not like most books. It has a unique "self-paced" format that encourages a reader to become personally involved. Designed to be "read with a pencil," there are an abundance of exercises, activities, assessments and cases that invite participation.

The objective of this book is to help a person develop a personal action plan to improve the quality of his or her emotional health, and then make any required behavioral changes to apply concepts presented in this book to that person's unique situation.

Managing Stress for Mental Fitness (and the other self-improvement books listed in the back of this book) can be used effectively in a number of ways. Here are some possibilities:

— Individual Study. Because the book is self-instructional, all that is needed is a quiet place, some time and a pencil. Completing the activities and exercises should provide not only valuable feedback but also practical ideas about steps for self-improvement.

— Workshops and Seminars. This book is ideal for pre-assigned reading prior to a workshop or seminar. With the basics in hand, the quality of participation should improve. More time can be spent on concept extensions and applications during the program. The book is also effective when distributed at the beginning of a session.

— Remote Location Training. Copies can be sent to those not able to attend "home office" training sessions.

— Informal Study Groups. Thanks to the format, brevity and low cost, this book is ideal for "brown-bag" or other informal group sessions.

There are other possibilities that depend on the objectives of the user. One thing for sure, even after it has been read, this book will serve as excellent reference material which can be easily reviewed. Good luck!

CONTENTS

SECTION I — UNDERSTANDING STRESS

SECTION II — LEARNING TO MANAGE STRESS

SECTION III — UNDERSTANDING SELF AND OTHERS

SECTION IV — UNDERSTANDING MENTAL HEALTH

SECTION V — MAINTAINING GOOD MENTAL HEALTH

SECTION *I*

UNDERSTANDING STRESS

STRESS IS DETERMINED BY THE BEHOLDER

Stress is a part of life. Life today is complex, and it is impossible to avoid stress. How much stress a person encounters and how she or he deals with it frequently has a direct connection with mental health. This section will look at stress and its many interesting dimensions, and will address strategies for change.

Stress is what we experience internally in response to a situation we find hard to deal with. Most of us handle routine stress readily. In other words, we are able to ''handle the situation.'' We can resolve our feelings and dissipate the tension. What is stressful for one person, however, may not be for another. In this sense, it may be counterproductive to tell someone not to worry about a situation if you do not consider the same situation as stressful. We all react to situations differently; it is part of being human.

Stress is a learning laboratory that constantly teaches us about how to successfully handle the difficulties we encounter in life. In the same way that exercising keeps our bodies physically fit, dealing effectively with the demands that affect our emotions keeps us mentally fit.

Anxiety is a signal that we are under stress. If this feeling keeps recurring, stress is not being dealt with effectively. For example, if you find yourself continually upset and angry, it would be worthwhile to determine the source of your anger and then find some appropriate way to deal with it. Otherwise your feelings will build and produce negative effects.

When our feelings build beyond a certain point, we begin to experience strain. If the situation we find troublesome disappears, the feeling of stress goes away. If the pressure does not let up, we eventually will show signs of mental and physical exhaustion.

Stress is essentially within us even though we may perceive it as coming from outside. It is important to recognize that not everyone experiences the same circumstances as stressful.

Expected "life events" that we all encounter are often stressful. These events include the entire range of experiences: a new birth; entering school; marriage; divorce; the loss of a family member, etc.

Sudden, unexpected catastrophic events are well-known causes of stress. Situations that result in our chronically feeling bad, either about ourselves or others, also can result in stress.

Expressing emotions is often difficult. The ability to recognize stress, and then learn to manage it through an appropriate expression of emotions, is extremely important when personally coping with stress.

People who continually hold their emotions inside often "boil over" at inappropriate times. This may damage their relationships with others. This seems to occur most often where stress has built up over a period of time. One way to help avoid this is to talk things over before the "boiling point" is reached.

STRESS MEANS DIFFERENT THINGS

People think about stress in different ways. For some, stress is related to a set of feelings that gives them an awareness that ''something is not right.'' For others, stress is basically a series of stressful events. These are predictable events based on the fact that the human experience includes a whole variety of life events that have significant meaning. For others, stress might be more accurately identified as a lifestyle. This lifestyle involves an intensive drive that ultimately affects us and others. Additionally, some see stress as the resulting physical symptoms, including ulcers, heart attacks, hypertension, etc. Being able to recognize that all of the above items describe the same process is helpful in understanding stress.

Below are some examples of the various ways to identify stress:

FEELINGS	CRISIS EVENTS
Restlessness	Death of Family Member
Keyed Up Feeling	Divorce
Anxiety	Separation
Depression	Business Failure
LIFESTYLE	**PHYSICAL SYMPTOMS**
Intensive Drive	Ulcers
Aggressiveness	Migraines
Time Urgency	Hypertension
Impatience	Heart Attack
Guilty When Not Working	Headaches
	Stroke

STRESS
IS IT GETTING YOU DOWN?

Our lives are filled with both happy and sad events. Many of us do not realize, however, that all of life's changes can result in stress on both our physical and mental health.

Below is a list of changes that occur in everyone's life. Some are everyday experiences. Others are not-so-common experiences. All can cause stress and anxiety.

The list on the facing page is a stress test that was developed by Drs. Thomas H. Holmes and Richard H. Rahe to help people understand what causes stress in their lives. Check each event that you have experienced in the last year and then add the attached point values. If you have a score of less than 150, you have only a 37 percent chance of getting sick within the next two years. Should your score be between 150 and 300, your chances of an illness increase to over 50 percent.

THE FOGGERTY REPORT, SIR? IT'S ON MY DESK...
YESSIR, SO IS THE HENDERSON FILE... ON MY DESK...
...UH-HUH, THAT'S ON MY DESK, TOO... RIGHT HERE.
MY DESK, SIR? NORMAL SIZE...WHY DO YOU ASK?

TEST YOURSELF

HOLMES-RAHE STRESS TEST

RANK EVENT	VALUE	YOUR SCORE
1. Death of spouse	100	___
2. Divorce	73	___
3. Marital separation	65	___
4. Jail term	63	___
5. Death of close family member	63	___
6. Personal injury or illness	53	___
7. Marriage	50	___
8. Fired from work	47	___
9. Marital reconciliation	45	___
10. Retirement	45	___
11. Change in family member's health	44	___
12. Pregnancy	40	___
13. Sex difficulties	39	___
14. Addition to family	39	___
15. Business readjustment	39	___
16. Change in financial status	38	___
17. Death of close friend	37	___
18. Change in number of marital arguments	35	___
19. Mortgage or loan over $10,000	31	___
20. Foreclosure of mortgage or loan	30	___
21. Change in work responsibilities	29	___
22. Son or daughter leaving home	29	___
23. Trouble with in-laws	29	___
24. Outstanding personal achievement	28	___
25. Spouse begins or starts work	26	___
26. Starting or finishing school	26	___
27. Change in living conditions	25	___
28. Revision of personal habits	24	___
29. Trouble with boss	23	___
30. Change in work hours, conditions	20	___
31. Change in residence	20	___
32. Change in schools	20	___
33. Change recreational habits	19	___
34. Change in church activities	19	___
35. Change in social activities	18	___
36. Mortgage or loan under $10,000	18	___
37. Change in sleeping habits	16	___
38. Change in number of family gatherings	15	___
39. Change in eating habits	14	___
40. Vacation	13	___
41. Christmas season	12	___
42. Minor violation of the law	11	___
TOTAL		___

SCORING: Add up the point values of all the items checked. If your score is 300 or more, you stand an almost 80 percent chance of getting sick in the near future as a result of the events. If your score is 150 to 299, the chances are about 50 percent. Less than 150, about 30 percent. This scale suggests that change in one's life requires an effort to adapt and then to regain stability. This process probably saps energy the body would ordinarily use to maintain itself, so susceptibility to illness increases. Reprinted with permission from the *Journal of Psychosomatic Research* (vol. II) by Thomas H. Holmes and Richard R. Rahe (Pergamon Press, 1967).

Type A behavior has been described by researchers Friedman and Rosenman as the kind of stressful lifestyle that more likely leads to heart attacks. On the other hand, recent research suggests Type A individuals may be better prepared to survive a heart attack when it does occur.

We know, however, that it is possible to modify our behavior and make a significant difference in our risk for potential heart attacks.

Type B behavior is more relaxed and seems to produce fewer physical problems related to stress.

On the following page are ten statements. If you check more boxes under #1 (usually) you tend to be more like Type A. If you check more boxes under #5 (seldom) you tend to be a Type B.

ARE YOU A:

TYPE A
or
TYPE B?

BEHAVIOR PATTERNS*

(Check the column most descriptive of your behavior.)

	Usually			Seldom	
	1	2	3	4	5
1. Do you move, walk, eat rapidly?					
2. Do you feel impatience with the rate most events take place?					
3. Do you attempt to finish the sentences of persons speaking to you?					
4. Do you become irritated or even enraged when a car ahead in your lane runs at a pace you consider too slow?					
5. Do you find it uncomfortable to watch others perform tasks you know you can do faster?					
6. Do you find it difficult to be interested in others' conversations if the subject is not of special interest to you?					
7. Do you feel vaguely guilty when you do nothing for several hours or several days?					
8. Do you schedule more than is possible to accomplish in a given time span?					
9. Do you believe that whatever your success may be, it is because of your ability to get things done faster than others?					
10. Do you frequently clench your fist or bang your hand on the table to confirm your point during conversation?					

*Adapted from *Type A Behavior and Your Heart,* by Meyer Friedman & Ray H. Rosenman (New York: Fawcett Crest, 1974). Reproduced by permission.

ADD BALANCE TO YOUR LIFE

Interestingly, Type B people rise to the "top" as frequently as do Type A's. Type B's tend to be less pressured and often deal with others more easily. They also seem to enjoy the little things in life that add meaning.

Having a plan for a balanced lifestyle is important. Such a plan will take into account the need for work and play; for regular exercise; for diet control; for relaxation; and for building positive relationships. These items will help you reduce stress and improve your mental health.

Later in this book you will have an opportunity to develop an action plan to help you achieve a more balanced lifestyle.

STAGES OF STRESS

It is natural to resist or deny the presence of stress. We all have a tendency to "plunge on," working harder and harder to overcome stressful situations rather than to acknowledge the situation and "back off." For example, sometimes in a stressful work environment, a person will return to the office night after night in an effort to deal with the stress. There comes a point when the mind and the body simply become exhausted. When this happens, efficiency decreases. Often, taking a break (i.e., doing something else, or getting away from the work) may be the most helpful way to relieve the stress.

Learning to identify the symptoms of stress and to recognize when resistance or denial is not helpful is essential. If we continue to experience stress and do nothing to alter the situation, it is likely we will develop physical problems such as exhaustion.

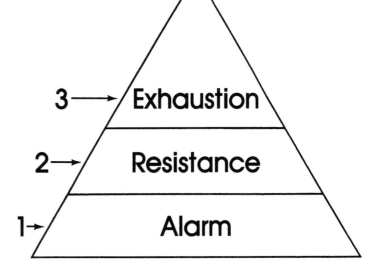

UNDERSTANDING THE THREE BASIC STAGES OF STRESS

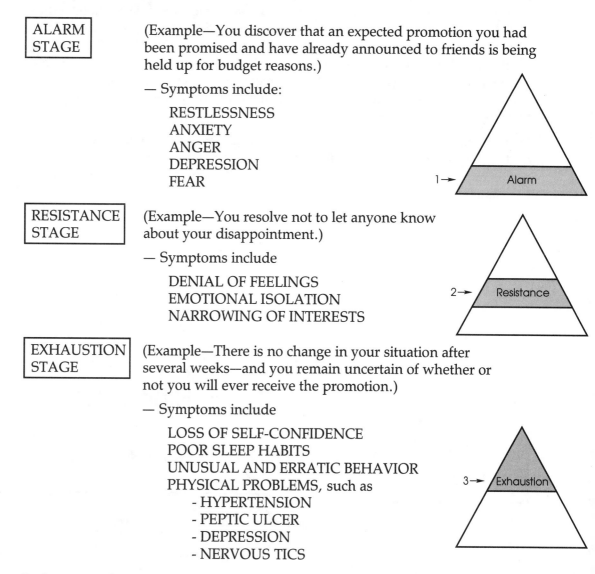

| ALARM STAGE | (Example—You discover that an expected promotion you had been promised and have already announced to friends is being held up for budget reasons.) |

— Symptoms include:

RESTLESSNESS
ANXIETY
ANGER
DEPRESSION
FEAR

1→ Alarm

| RESISTANCE STAGE | (Example—You resolve not to let anyone know about your disappointment.) |

— Symptoms include

DENIAL OF FEELINGS
EMOTIONAL ISOLATION
NARROWING OF INTERESTS

2→ Resistance

| EXHAUSTION STAGE | (Example—There is no change in your situation after several weeks—and you remain uncertain of whether or not you will ever receive the promotion.) |

— Symptoms include

LOSS OF SELF-CONFIDENCE
POOR SLEEP HABITS
UNUSUAL AND ERRATIC BEHAVIOR
PHYSICAL PROBLEMS, such as
   - HYPERTENSION
   - PEPTIC ULCER
   - DEPRESSION
   - NERVOUS TICS

3→ Exhaustion

In the stages described above, the impact of stress likely can be reduced by identifying and accepting (owning) the feelings of stage one, avoiding the isolation and withdrawal of stage two, and seeking medical and/or professional counseling for stage three.

Sharing your situation with another caring person and talking out your feelings may help give a new perspective.

Hans Selye, M.D., a foremost researcher in the field of stress, described three stages of stress in several of his writings, including *The Stress of Life,* revised edition (New York: McGraw-Hill, 1976).

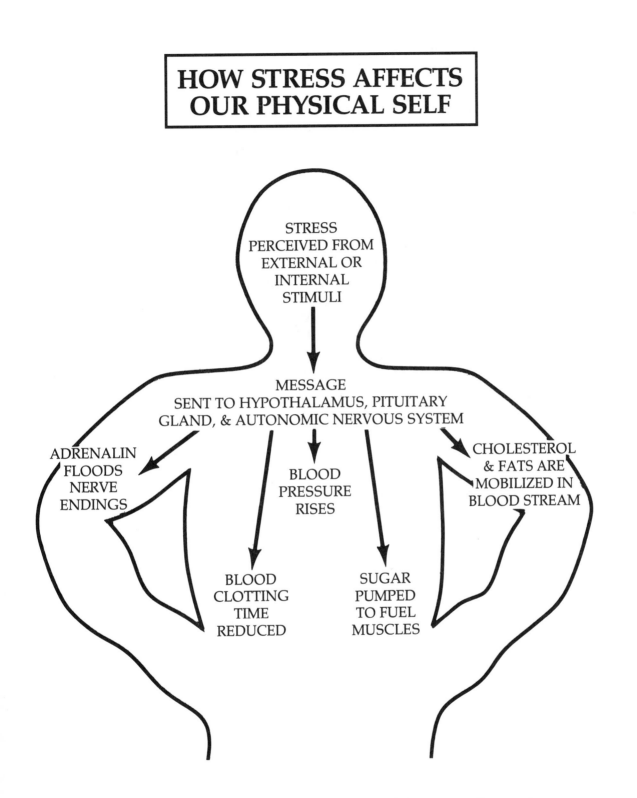

HOW STRESS AFFECTS OUR PHYSICAL SELF

STRESS
PERCEIVED FROM
EXTERNAL OR
INTERNAL
STIMULI

MESSAGE
SENT TO HYPOTHALAMUS, PITUITARY
GLAND, & AUTONOMIC NERVOUS SYSTEM

ADRENALIN
FLOODS
NERVE
ENDINGS

BLOOD
PRESSURE
RISES

CHOLESTEROL
& FATS ARE
MOBILIZED IN
BLOOD STREAM

BLOOD
CLOTTING
TIME
REDUCED

SUGAR
PUMPED
TO FUEL
MUSCLES

Continuous stress has been shown to have a gradual damaging effect on the circulatory system, digestive tract, lungs, muscles and/or joints. It also hastens the process of aging.

OUR "SYSTEM" UNDER STRESS

We believe that it is possible to live in stressful situations over a relatively long period of time *if* we can find ways to manage the stress. The diagram below suggests what happens as our system responds biochemically when we are under stress. We have all heard stories of people being able to "lift pianos" and do other wonderful and amazing feats under conditions of a house fire, automobile accident, etc.

While that "high-voltage" charge of chemicals in our system makes it possible for us to do incredible things, it also can be a kind of poison in our system if conditions stay at a peak indefinitely. Our task is to find a way, preferably something we can do daily, to restore our normal hormone balance. Finding our own best way to bring the stress level down, on a regular basis, is both a challenge and a discipline. We should also note that if we do not find that systematic way of bringing our stress level down to "normal," the tendency is for our system to simply adjust to being at the "high-voltage" level, which then becomes destructive to both our physical and emotional systems.

BLOODSTREAM FLOODED
WITH "HIGH-VOLTAGE" CHARGE OF CHEMICALS

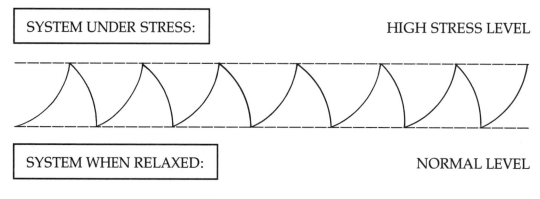

SYSTEM UNDER STRESS: HIGH STRESS LEVEL

SYSTEM WHEN RELAXED: NORMAL LEVEL

SYSTEM RETURNS TO NORMAL
HORMONE BALANCE

The goal is to return to a normal hormone level on a regular basis.

STRESS IN THE WORKPLACE

Understanding the many forms of stress has been the focus of this first section. Stress in the workplace is the topic in the second part of this chapter. Examining this issue from the perspectives of both a supervisor and an employee allows us to think about the important part both play in setting a climate for either creating or managing stress. It is important to recognize, however, that a certain amount of stress is necessary in order to get work done.

A supervisor needs to ask the question "What do I do or what should I do to create a less-stressful environment for my employees?" Some supervisors are referred to as "carriers of stress." This is the analogy to a carrier of a virus that can be spread among the population. As an employee, what can or should I do to create a less-stressful environment for myself and others?

If we can accept the notion that "I stress me" (meaning I allow others to stress me), then I am willing and able to look at issues that help me so that I might determine how best to deal with stress in the workplace.

JOB STRESS

Occupational stress is prevalent in most work situations. Today, it is unrealistic to expect that jobs are stress-free. However, if the organization's culture and the climate are such that both employer and employee are willing to work together in identifying stressful situations, stress *can* be minimized. Below are seven typical job stressors. Look at the list and add an additional three stressors that come from your own work experience. Rank them in descending order to determine the areas of stress most pertinent to you.

_____ 1. I am trapped in situations of conflict between people who expect different things of me.

_____ 2. I am overloaded—they assign more than can be done (or) more than can be done well and maintain my self-esteem.

_____ 3. I have ambiguous job responsibilities; I am not clear about the scope of my job.

_____ 4. I am insecure about venturing outside my normal job boundaries.

_____ 5. I have difficult bosses (or subordinates).

_____ 6. I worry over carrying responsibility for others.

_____ 7. I lack participation in decisions affecting my job.

_____ 8. _____

_____ 9. _____

_____ 10. _____

SYMPTOMS OF STRESS IN THE WORKPLACE

The symptoms below are suggested as being particularly helpful in diagnosing stress in the workplace. Add any additional symptoms from your own experience.

1. When events are faced with cynicism and negativism.

2. When the drive to pursue perfection pushes one beyond what is realistically possible.

3. When conflicts with spouse and family seem to be increasing without clear reasons.

4. When alcohol and/or other drugs become an escape from the pressures of the job.

5. When there is a tendency to bully and/or seek perfection from those one supervises.

6. When there is little time planned for anything except work.

7. When it seems impossible to relax or enjoy leisure activities because one's mind is constantly on work.

8. When one feels ill at ease in social situations that are not related to work.

9. _____

10. _____

ISSUES FOR MANAGERS AND SUPERVISORS

If you are a supervisor or manager, think about stress in your workplace, and as honestly as you can, respond to the questions below.

1. What kinds of stress do you encounter as a consequence of your lifestyle?

   _____

   _____

   _____

2. What kinds of stress do those you supervise encounter as a result of your lifestyle?

   _____

   _____

   _____

3. What do you do that creates a climate for reducing or increasing stress in your work situation?

   _____

   _____

   _____

4. How aware are you of the kinds of stresses that employees bring with them from home?

   _____

   _____

   _____

BURNOUT: AN OCCUPATIONAL HAZARD

Is the concept of burnout a scientific diagnosis, an excuse or a description of stressful conditions that have gone on too long? We would suggest the latter, because burnout is simply a description of the condition of people who have become discouraged, depressed or have developed a sense of hopelessness about being able to alleviate stress. Another way to think of burnout is as the logical conclusion of stress over a long period of time.

CONDITIONS LEADING TO BURNOUT

1. Unrealistically high expectations for oneself

2. A sense of powerlessness in being able to remedy problems in the workplace

3. Experiencing a lack of support or encouragement from supervisors

4. Preoccupation with work and putting in long hours to the exclusion of outside activities.

SYMPTOMS OF BURNOUT

1. Works long hours with an assumption that more time on the job will ease the stress

2. Exhaustion/fatigue—constantly feels tired and lacks energy

3. Dreads going to work each day

4. Loss of appetite, frequent illness and muscle tension

5. Bored and detached

6. Impatient and irritable with people at work and at home

7. Inability to concentrate and a decreasing quality of work

8. Negative, cynical and hostile attitudes toward others, particularly superiors

9. Loss of self-esteem and self-confidence

10. Blames someone else when things go wrong.

BURNOUT (continued)

WHO IS MOST LIKELY TO EXPERIENCE BURNOUT?

1. Administrators

2. Best employees; dedicated workaholics

3. Those in mid-years (dealing with unfulfilled dreams, living up to others' expectations, disillusioned about what life is all about)

4. Those who feel ''caught'' (feelings that are related to financial security, location changes, fear and/or the threat of unemployment).

THE MOST IMPORTANT ROLE FOR MANAGERS IN DEALING WITH BURNOUT

Managers should strive to create a climate within the work situation where:

1. Negative feelings can be expressed.

2. Supervisors are provided training and support.

3. An opportunity is provided to understand employees as people.

4. It is possible to achieve realistic goals.

5. The reward system includes recognition for achievement.

6. Possibilities for staff realignment make it possible for job change, either temporarily or by way of promotion.

7. A career counseling program allows employees to talk about their own career goals.

8. A continuing education plan is made a part of each employee's career objective. This allows for new knowledge, training and redirection in one's career.

SOME STRESS IS NECESSARY

While too much stress can have a negative personal impact, an appropriate amount of stress is an important part of being an effective person and employee. Without some stress, many of us would not bother to even get out of bed each morning. A certain amount of stress helps most of us stay on our toes and motivates us to achieve a standard of excellence that is a powerful step in promoting self-esteem. Finding a level of stress that is helpful in producing good results yet does not become debilitating is the goal.

The Yerkes-Dodson Law diagram below shows a bell curve that recognizes the stress level in one direction and efficiency or performance in the other. Each of us needs to find the level of stress that is most effective for becoming quality persons and quality employees. Optimum efficiency and optimum stress will vary for each of us, so there is no "right" standard. Finding our ideal is an important dimension so that we will be able to use the *appropriate* amount of stress in our lives.

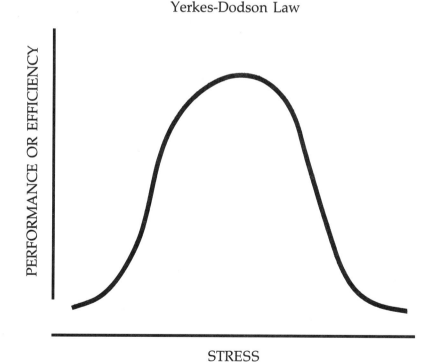

Yerkes-Dodson Law

PERFORMANCE OR EFFICIENCY

STRESS

SECTION *II*

LEARNING TO MANAGE STRESS

This section will give suggested strategies and specific methods to assess your own stress level and begin its management.

Taking responsibility for
your own stress is a
way of learning to manage
stress in your life.

WEEKLY STRESS JOURNAL

This exercise will help you begin tracing your stress levels to become more aware of the times, places and circumstances that contribute to stress in your life. You can make notes in the daily log. To keep the momentum in your writing, we suggest that you write no more than a brief paragraph for each day. Focus on who, what, when and where contributed to the stress in your life for that particular day. Then, to the right, on a scale of one to ten (one being relatively little stress to ten being relatively high stress), rate your day.

1   2   3   4   5   6   7   8   9   10

Sunday _____

_____

_____

Monday _____

_____

_____

Tuesday _____

_____

_____

Wednesday _____

_____

_____

Thursday _____

_____

_____

Friday _____

_____

_____

Saturday _____

_____

_____

After using your stress journal for a few weeks, you begin to get a fairly good pattern of where you need to focus the changes in your lifestyle.

STRESS CHARTING

As you keep your journal, you will begin to get a pattern of where the stress in your life is most significant. In this exercise, think of these four main quadrants in terms of how you experience stress as it relates to home-family, work, recreation and social life.

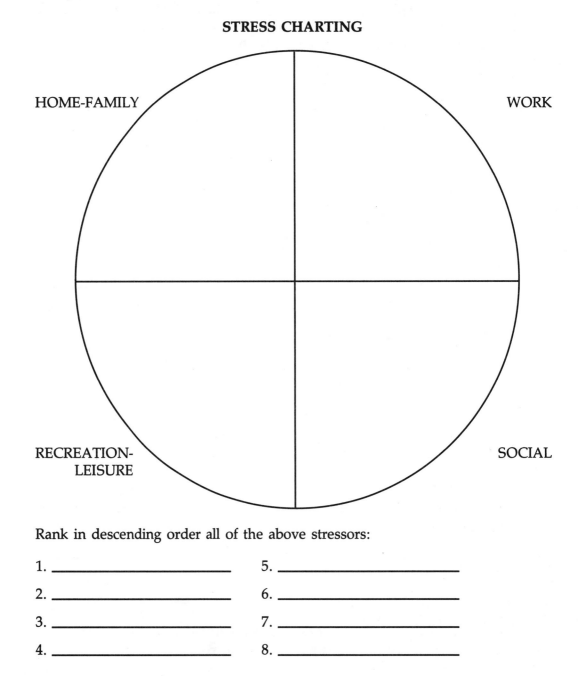

Rank in descending order all of the above stressors:

1. _____   5. _____

2. _____   6. _____

3. _____   7. _____

4. _____   8. _____

CONCEPTUAL METHODS OF COPING WITH STRESS

1. *Change your internal attitudes/perceptions.* While we may not be able to change some types of external stimuli that are stressful, we *can* change our internal attitudes and perceptions of these stresses. Examples include:

   - Develop social supports that reduce your sense of aloneness.
   - Develop a sense of humor about your situation.
   - Talk about troubles with friends.
   - Seek professional counseling.
   - Own your personal stress.
   - Know yourself and your level of optimum stress.
   - Balance work and play.

2. *Change your interaction with the environment.* This strategy says that if we can "work smarter, not harder," we may be able to reduce the amount of stress on us.

   - Improve your skills in areas like goal setting, time management and conflict management.
   - Take assertiveness training.
   - Use peer feedback as a way to identify areas for possible changes in functioning.
   - Use a case consultant for particularly difficult job areas.
   - Slow down.

3. *Change your physical ability to cope.* The most common stress reduction activities are those designed to improve the physical resources of our body to handle the stress that we experience.

   - Get adequate and proper nutrition.
   - Implement a fitness program.
   - Cut down on intake stressors (i.e., caffeine, nicotine, sugar, etc.).
   - Relax, learn to loaf a little.
   - Get enough sleep and rest.
   - Develop some recreational activities.

4. *Change your environment.* If a stressor is closely related to a particular environment, find a way to place yourself in a different environment. Caution should be taken that one does not develop the style of avoiding all stressful situations, but sometimes this may be a good short-term solution. For example:

   - Quit going to certain meetings.
   - Change job/vocation/location.
   - Develop extended education programs.
   - Structure time off from work.
   - Set up your job, if possible, so you can work in a variety of different program areas.

STRATEGIES FOR SUPERVISORS TO HELP EMPLOYEES MANAGE STRESS

1. Outline goals clearly to workers and provide timely feedback on achievement.

2. Be sure instructions are clear.

3. Evaluate completion deadlines; are they reasonable?

4. Eliminate conflict between your demands and other supervisors' demands.

5. Deal with personality conflicts directly before they demoralize the rest of the group.

6. Have regular work reviews to provide accurate and timely feedback.

7. Give reassurance that good work is noted and appreciated.

8. Have workers participate, as much as possible, in decisions that affect their work.

9. Have a career development program that helps employees look at the reality of their job and the possibilities within their job situation.

10. Have a well-functioning employee assistance program for recognizing and dealing with specific employee stressors.

STRATEGIES FOR EMPLOYEES FOR MANAGING JOB STRESS

1. Clarify organization mission and goals.

2. Be orderly in work habits.

3. Determine priorities and stick with them.

4. Make a daily "to do" list to keep on track.

5. Don't wait until the deadline.

6. Stick with a decision once it is made. Don't continue to worry about whether you might have done better.

7. Admit your mistakes. Don't try to cover up. Do what you need to correct the mistakes, then get on with other tasks.

EXPRESS YOUR FEELINGS AND DEAL WITH STRESS

Expressing your feelings is perhaps the best way to relieve the pressure that we call stress. Putting your feelings into words is often the key. This is in contrast to keeping feelings bottled up. Finding the best way to appropriately and constructively express your feelings is a useful learning experience.

Expressing your emotions can take many forms. Below are some constructive ideas. Review this list and check those that fall within your comfort zone. Then, rank in order the top five ways in which you prefer to express your feelings. Add your own stress relievers before a final ranking.

☐ Talk with your spouse or significant other.

☐ Talk with a good friend.

☐ Join a small sharing group.

☐ Use a tape recorder to verbalize feelings.

☐ Talk with a clergy person, counselor or therapist.

☐ Write letters to friends.

☐ Keep a journal describing your feelings.

☐ Talk with your supervisor at work.

☐ Have a family discussion.

☐ Exercise vigorously.

☐ _____

☐ _____

☐ _____

☐ _____

☐ _____

STRESS RELEASES AND SAFETY VALVES

Place a check in the appropriate column. Try to be completely honest.

I do well	I'm average	Need to improve
5	3	1

I'm succeeding at:

____ ____ ____   1. "Owning" my own stress (not blaming others)

____ ____ ____   2. Knowing my level of optimum stress (the level of stress that allows you to do your best without becoming destructive)

____ ____ ____   3. Balancing work and play (scheduling time for play)

____ ____ ____   4. Loafing more (learning to do nothing at times and feel okay about it)

____ ____ ____   5. Getting enough sleep and rest rather than ending up with what is left over at the end of the day (scheduling adequate sleep)

____ ____ ____   6. Refusing to take on more than I can handle (learning to say no)

____ ____ ____   7. Working off tension (hard physical effort on a regular basis)

____ ____ ____   8. Setting realistic goals (goals that can be achieved within a reasonable time frame)

____ ____ ____   9. Practicing relaxation (meditating with music or biofeedback)

____ ____ ____   10. Slowing down (taking pleasure in every moment rather than rushing through life)

____ ____ ____   11. Putting emphasis on *being* rather than on *doing* (Being a person others like to be around is more important than "doing" many activities.)

32

I do well	I'm average	Need to improve
5	**3**	**1**

____ ____ ____ 12. Managing my time, including planning for time alone (setting priorities and doing those things that are most important)

____ ____ ____ 13. Planning regular recreation (Recreation is a complete change of pace and something that is fun to do.)

____ ____ ____ 14. Having a physical fitness program (having a specific plan for strenuous exercise)

____ ____ ____ 15. Avoiding too much caffeine (limiting coffee and cola drinks)

____ ____ ____ 16. Emphasizing good nutrition in diet (learning about nutrition and avoiding junk foods)

____ ____ ____ 17. Avoiding alcohol or other chemicals to deal with pressure (Dependency on alcohol or drugs deals with symptoms rather than the problem.)

____ ____ ____ 18. Avoiding emotional "overload" (Taking on problems of others when you are under stress is destructive.)

____ ____ ____ 19. Selecting emotional "investments" more carefully (things we can get involved with that call for emotional involvement—it is necessary to choose these carefully)

____ ____ ____ 20. Giving and accepting positive "strokes" (Being able to express positive things to others and receive positive comments in return is an achievement.)

____ ____ ____ 21. Talking out troubles and getting professional help if needed (Being willing to seek help is a sign of strength rather than weakness.)

____ ____ ____ Total checks in each column

Multiply	Multiply	Multiply
X	X	X
5	3	1

____ ____ ____ **TOTAL SCORE** (add columns and see scale on facing page)

SCORE YOURSELF

If you scored between 21 and 50, there are several areas you need to develop to better release your stress. It might be a good idea to discuss some of your answers with a counselor or close friend.

If you scored between 51 and 75, you have discovered a variety of ways to deal effectively with stress. Make a note of those items you checked "need to improve" and work on strategies to help you move to the "I'm Average" box.

If your score was 75 or greater — congratulations. You apparently have found some excellent ways to deal with frustration and the complexities of life. Stay alert to protect the valuable skills you have acquired.

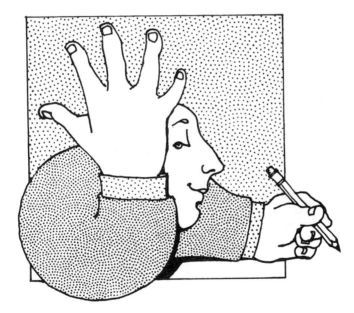

REVIEW THIS BOOK LATER AND RATE YOURSELF AGAIN.

Case studies provide an opportunity to see how others cope with life situations similar to those we have experienced. Four case studies are included in this book.

CASE STUDY #1

After reading the case study on the facing page, make an assessment of the situation-and recommend some "safety valves" for Maria.

CASE STUDY #1
MARIA COPES WITH STRESS

Maria is a divorcee who is raising two young children while also working full-time as a legal secretary in a well-known law firm. Following her divorce, Maria went back to school to acquire skills for a job that would pay enough to support herself and her children.

Maria's daily routine seems increasingly overwhelming. She gets up at 5:30 a.m. to prepare breakfast, make lunches and do laundry, so clean clothes are available for the family. At 7:30 she drops Jose, age 2, at the babysitter and takes daughter Carla, age 7, to school. (Carla's school is 10 miles in the opposite direction from where Maria works.)

At work, Maria is expected to be on time and deliver high-quality output. Yet when there are even simple problems with the children, it is difficult for her to get to work on time. When they are sick, Maria feels the need to take time off. Her boss is very demanding, and when he is under pressure, he expects her to work overtime or take work home.

To compound things, Maria has been taking an advanced course in word processing two nights a week so she will be prepared to improve her financial position as the children get older. The course work adds to her stress.

In summary, Maria's day is filled with stress from morning until she goes to bed at night. She has little time for herself, and doesn't see much hope for change in the next several years.

What is likely to happen if nothing changes this picture? What ''safety valves'' would you suggest?

_____

_____

_____

_____

_____

(For the authors' views, see page 85.)

SECTION *III*

UNDERSTANDING YOURSELF AND OTHERS

As humans, we all face problems. Understanding yourself and the things that trouble you most is an important step in solving your life's problems.

Our mental health is often determined by the way we work with and relate to others.

The more a person isolates him/herself, the more difficult it is to enjoy good mental health.

RELATING TO OTHERS

The purpose of this scale is to assess your style of relating to others. Be honest.

Others would say that I:

	Usually	Occasionally	Seldom
1. Communicate easily and clearly with people			
2. Am a good listener			
3. Am assertive in my communication without being critical or negative			
4. Have considerable self-confidence when relating to others			
5. Am willing to discuss feelings with others			
6. Am able to face conflict and handle antagonism			
7. Can resolve interpersonal problems between myself and others			
8. Am able to accept expressions of warmth from friends			
9. Trust other people			
10. Will often constructively influence peers			
11. Can assume responsibility for any difficulties with others			
12. Am open-minded when discussing important issues			
13. Encourage feedback from others about my behavior			
14. Am relatively free of prejudice			
15. Am open and easy to get to know.			

If you answered ''usually'' to ten of the above, you appear to have good relationships with others. If you answered ''occasionally'' to five or more, it may be an indication you need to focus more on this area. If you answered ''seldom'' to any question — this is an excellent place to begin working on some self-improvement.

ACCEPTING MYSELF AS A UNIQUE PERSON

In this competitive world there is often pressure to "be like somebody else." We may have grown up with the feeling that we are not acceptable the way we are. If prolonged, these feelings can develop into a poor self-image.

Learning to accept oneself as is and to make the most of that self is an important step toward good mental health.

When you identify your uniqueness and are willing to enhance or modify your good qualities, you are on the right track.

UNIQUENESS EXERCISE AHEAD

I AM UNIQUE

To help you identify your unique qualities, there are three blocks below. In the first block list the names of people you see being similar to you and make a note of the similarities. In block #2 list traits in those same people that you see as different, and state in what ways they are different. Finally, identify three characteristics that are uniquely you (block #3), and briefly describe how each characteristic is or can be an asset to your future development.

#1 SIMILAR

1. _____
   name   ways similar

2. _____

3. _____

#2 DIFFERENT

1. _____
   name   ways different

2. _____

3. _____

#3 UNIQUELY ME

1. _____
   characteristic   why an asset

2. _____

3. _____

In what ways can my uniqueness become an asset?

_____

_____

_____

False assumptions about individuals can produce unrealistic expectations. Sorting out what is realistic and unrealistic is an important part of growth. For example, some people are more sensitive than others and become depressed if there is any criticism or indication they are not appreciated by everyone. This is an example of a false assumption that can lead to emotional stress. In reality, if a person is making a contribution of any kind, not everyone will appreciate that contribution equally.

UNREALISTIC EXPECTATIONS

Ten false assumptions that work against understanding myself and my relationships with others:

1. That it is possible for everybody to like me

2. That I must be competent and adequate all of the time

3. That other people are bad if they do not share my values

4. That ''all is lost'' when I get treated unfairly or experience rejection

5. That I cannot control or change my feelings

6. That unless everything is structured and understandable, there is reason to be fearful or anxious

7. That problems of the past that have influenced my life must continue to determine my feelings and behavior

8. That it is easier to avoid problems than to accept them and begin working toward a solution

9. That life should be better than it is

10. That health and happiness can be realized by waiting for somebody else to make something happen.

Do any of these sound familiar? In the space provided, write a brief statement about any of the ten that have caused you the most difficulty.

_____

_____

_____

_____

44

We have more strengths than we often realize. Others may see strengths in us that we minimize or do not recognize. There is also a tendency for some incongruity between what we feel is a strength and what we perceive others feel.

The facing page provides space to assess your strengths as *you* see them as well as how you perceive *others* see them.

An example of someone who underestimates his or her strengths is a person who cannot accept praise without needing to negate it in some way. This same person is not likely to accept a challenging assignment because of an underlying fear that he or she is not capable and would not do a satisfactory job.

ASSESSING MY STRENGTHS

Write brief statements about the following. Be realistic and honest.

1. Things I feel I do well:

_____

_____

_____

_____

_____

2. Things other people consider as my strengths:

_____

_____

_____

_____

_____

3. Things I can do for others to help them recognize and realize *their* strengths.

_____

_____

_____

_____

_____

Understanding the basic needs of others will help you understand how to better relate to them. Human relationships are developed when people give and receive freely to and from each other. Relationships that develop when only one person's needs are being met tend to be shallow and short-lived.

Knowing that others need to feel important, need to be appreciated, and need to have others interested in them is essential to building good human relationships.

UNIVERSAL HUMAN NEEDS

Human beings have many needs. When met, these needs help people stay emotionally healthy. A list is presented below. Add to this list any of your needs that are missing and then rank them in order, with number one being your *most* important need.

Needs everyone has:

Rank Order

_____ The need to feel important to one's self and in the eyes of others

_____ The need to be perceived as successful by self and others

_____ The need to be needed and/or wanted

_____ The need to feel useful

_____ The need to be loved, appreciated, accepted and/or recognized by others

_____ The need to feel influential

_____ The need to belong to something bigger than self

_____ The need to experience growth in skills or learning

_____ The need for adventure.

Others:

_____ _____

_____ _____

_____ _____

_____ _____

48

Understanding and accepting yourself is the first step toward relating successfully to others!

During counseling, it is not uncommon to encounter individuals who are obsessed with a distorted assumption that friends and family do not like them. A significant event in the counseling process is when these individuals become aware that it is they who do not like or accept themselves.

The underlying feelings of those who have a difficult time accepting themselves often cause feelings of personal unworthiness to be projected to others.

BUILDING BETTER RELATIONSHIPS

Circle the number that best represents the way you relate to others.

I don't listen to what is really being said.	1	2	3	4	5	I listen with genuine interest.
I cut people off in conversation.	1	2	3	4	5	I let people finish before jumping in with my thoughts.
I make judgments about people before getting to know them.	1	2	3	4	5	I do not let first impressions determine a relationship.
I am not interested in other people's problems or ideas.	1	2	3	4	5	I devote attention to other people before immediately telling about myself.
I have no interest in the success of others.	1	2	3	4	5	I can honestly compliment and encourage the success of others.
I am unable to tolerate joking and kidding by others.	1	2	3	4	5	I am able to enjoy all forms of humor.
I discourage opinions that differ from my own.	1	2	3	4	5	I respond to new ideas with enthusiasm.
I show impatience with others in nonverbal ways that express disapproval.	1	2	3	4	5	My body language shows approval of others.

(If you have more 1's and 2's than 4's and 5's, this may be an indication that you need additional work in learning to work with others.)

Frequently we get into patterns of relating that are not satisfying, yet we are unable to change a pattern because it is so much a part of us.

Being aware of how we relate to family and friends is an important first step.

Recognizing that we can change patterns that have brought us difficulties in the past is the second step.

On the facing page are typical patterns that lead to relationship difficulties.

Poor interpersonal habits are like old friends-they are hard to give up.

NEGATIVE PATTERNS IN INTERPERSONAL RELATIONSHIPS

Interacting with people can be either an experience that produces negative feelings or a positive one that produces good feelings.

The ability to build warm and supportive relationships, without giving up integrity or identity, is essential. Being able to say, "I disagree with you but will explore other alternatives," is a healthy approach.

Following are interpersonal relationship patterns to be avoided:

1. Do not relate to others by automatically placing them in "boxes." This does not allow much opportunity to get to know a person as a unique individual. For example, you may think, "I do not like Alice because she lives in a poor part of town." You have put Alice in a negative box without relating to her as a person.

2. Combative styles in relationships should be avoided. Relationships often become strained when there is a tendency to be argumentative and rigid. While some people enjoy arguing, most do not. If you set up disagreements in your conversations, people will learn to avoid you rather than enter a "contest" of wills every time they talk with you.

3. It is equally annoying to be so agreeable that you don't seem to have unique qualities. If you tend to be smiley and without an opinion, even when you disagree on a serious subject, people will discredit your willingness to speak your feelings and may begin to distrust you.

Which of the above most closely resembles you? Jot your response below, and explain your reasons. Are there any other negative patterns in your "interpersonal style"?

_____

_____

_____

_____

_____

_____

Becoming more aware of oneself helps one to understand why relationships are sometimes difficult. Accepting responsibility for conflicts and interpersonal problems is an important first step toward positive change.

CASE STUDY #2

CASE STUDY #2
JOHN RELATES TO
FAMILY AND FRIENDS

John, age 37, is a construction worker. He and his wife, Shirley, have four children, the youngest of whom is a high school junior. John frequently has conflicts on the job and at home. He does not know why he becomes involved with other people to the point of getting into an argument. He often winds up alienating people who could be his friends. He feels upset with himself after arguing with his wife or a family member when he or she tries to communicate with him.

John is vaguely aware that he has not been promoted because of his inability to get along with co-workers. Also, he recently was threatened with divorce by his wife after an especially intense argument. His relationship with the children, which has never been strong, has deteriorated. His family views John as extremely judgmental and critical. To avoid constant arguments, his family and friends tend to stay away from him.

John has difficulty understanding himself, and even more difficulty understanding his trouble of getting along with others. Things have reached a point where he genuinely wants help to try to correct some of his problems.

What do you think are his chances for significant change? What suggestions would you make?

_____

_____

_____

_____

_____

_____

(For the authors' views, see page 85.)

SECTION *IV*

UNDERSTANDING MENTAL HEALTH

In its simplest form, mental health is the capacity to work (be productive), to love (have friends) and to play (renew one's self) with relative freedom from internal stress and without causing stress to others.

In another sense, mental health is the capacity to cope with all of life, including its joys and sorrows.

Do you consider yourself a mentally healthy person?

BASIC INGREDIENTS FOR GOOD MENTAL HEALTH

To understand mental health, it is important to recognize some of the concepts related to emotional maturity. Below are criteria that describe an emotionally mature person. Check those statements you feel are like you.

An emotionally mature person . . .

_____ 1. Can fully experience the entire range of human emotions

_____ 2. Is able to develop and maintain satisfying relationships with others

_____ 3. Sees life as a learning experience that can bring rewards from experience

_____ 4. Is free from debilitating fears that unduly restrict risk taking in life

_____ 5. Can accept unchangeable reality and make the most of the situation

_____ 6. Can accept him or herself in a realistic way

_____ 7. Is relatively free from prejudice and able to accept differences in others

_____ 8. Is non-blaming of others and is willing to assume personal responsibility

_____ 9. Is able to accept emotional support _from_ others as well as appropriately express feelings that give support _to_ others

_____ 10. Can rebound from life's crises without prolonged feelings of stress, grief or guilt.

If you were able to check five or more items, you are on your way to emotional maturity. None of us ever achieves total maturity, so don't be discouraged if you did not check all ten statements. Understand that life is an opportunity to learn and grow.

EMOTIONS AND YOU

Fear, anger, joy,
grief, jealousy, love,
anxiety and depression
are common human emotions.

The emotionally mature
person learns to express
these emotions appropriately.

MENTAL HEALTH AND EMOTIONS

To a great degree, mental health is related to how well you manage your emotions. This includes both feeling good about yourself as well as feeling good about interactions with your family, friends, colleagues and co-workers. The ability to experience and express emotions is uniquely human. Our emotional make-up is that part of us that contributes to the elation of great joy or the depths of profound sorrow. Emotional adjustment also contributes to maintaining an evenness through the ups and downs of life without the demands of experiencing continual extreme highs and/or lows. Emotions also warn us of danger and give us a way to express and receive love and affection as well as anger and sorrow.

Most of us know that when we get physically sick it is usually best to visit a medical doctor. This person can prescribe treatment that usually alleviates the problem. Thus, physical illness has a fairly direct relationship between symptom and cure. The world of emotions is far more complex. For example, many of us have been taught not to show our emotions. Others somehow have learned that we should not even have emotions (feelings) about certain events. Males in particular have frequently received messages from parents and/or society that ''real men'' should strictly control their emotions. The assumption is that the world is better dealt with on the basis of logic rather than feelings.

Emotions are the feelings associated with all of the events and activities in our lives. For example, most people feel grief when a loved one dies. These feelings are normal, and when experienced fully, they allow the mourner to adapt to the loss. If we do not know how to experience these feelings satisfactorily, despair may overtake us. Instead of healing the sense of loss, it may cause depression that can become chronic and incapacitating.

By way of another example, children who are victimized by physical and/or sexual abuse often carry the scars and stigma of such experiences into adult life. These ''scars'' affect the capacity both to express feelings to others as well as to receive similar feelings in return. Often a layer of guilt, although unfounded, is part of the complex emotional problems that persist into adulthood.

All of us deal with our emotions either destructively or constructively. For some, bottling up of emotions may result in various physical problems. For others, the expression of emotions may be inappropriate for the time or situation and result in negative feedback.

In summary, understanding your emotions and learning how to express your feelings appropriately are signs of emotional maturity.

LOOKING AT MY MENTAL HEALTH

On the facing page is an opportunity to review how well you understand the basic rules of mental health. Don't worry if the questions seem new or strange, or if you have difficulty with the answers. This is simply a quick way to introduce you to concepts that will be explored further in this book.

LOOKING AT MYSELF

One of the most difficult aspects of developing and maintaining mental health is being able to look at oneself objectively.

A necessary first step is a willingness to explore feelings about yourself and how you relate to others. Learning about self can be an exciting adventure or journey. Each discovery can open up new possibilities for growth. As you learn more about yourself, you may learn to realistically accept limitations, or begin to see some previously unrecognized potential.

Learning to maximize your potential, once it is discovered, is what makes life challenging and exciting.

HOW IS YOUR MENTAL HEALTH?

Everyone has a combination of emotions, attitudes and behaviors which creates a unique personality. You have considerable control over the items that make up your personality.

Below is a "pre-test" that will help you identify several key issues related to mental or emotional health. Circle the answer that best describes you. Please be as honest as possible.

My friends would agree that:

1.	I am basically a pessimistic person.	True	False
2.	I frequently wish I were somebody else or had another person's qualities.	True	False
3.	I find myself frequently angry at people.	True	False
4.	I tend to blame others for my problems.	True	False
5.	I often assume blame for other people's problems.	True	False
6.	I find it difficult to encourage and support the successes of others.	True	False
7.	It is hard for me to accept encouragement and support from friends or family.	True	False
8.	I do not have many friends.	True	False
9.	I worry constantly about things I cannot change.	True	False
10.	I am frightened about things others do not seem to be concerned about.	True	False

> If you answered true to five or more statements, now is a good time to review your approach to life. This book can help you do that.

This third case study (on the facing page) discusses some of the issues we have covered so far.

Try to anticipate the emotional implications of this case and suggest what can or should be done.

Try to relate this, and all of the cases, to your own situation.

CASE #3

CASE STUDY #3
ROGER DEALS WITH A
COMMON PROBLEM

Roger is a young man who recently completed college. He selected a major he liked, and his grades were above average. By all of the usual standards he should be a happy person. As the youngest member of a high-achieving family (where all members have become successful business or professional people), Roger feels considerable pressure to succeed. Roger is also contemplating marriage to a long-time girlfriend, and this has increased the pressure.

Roger sometimes feels overwhelmed about the future. Recently, he has been spending more and more time alone. His friends are starting to see him as preoccupied and moody. For the first time in his life, he finds it difficult to make decisions about the future.

Although he feels it would be difficult to discuss with friends, Roger is worried about his family's high expectations. He is uneasy that he will not measure up to the success of his brothers and sisters. Now that the college routine is over, he is unsettled about the future and his lack of structure.

Unfortunately, Roger has been conditioned to think that real men do not express their feelings. He has approached his present situation by trying not to let anybody know how he is feeling inside. In fact, much of the time he really isn't sure what he is feeling. He is spending more and more time alone.

What is likely to happen to Roger in terms of behavior and feelings if he doesn't find a way to come out of his shell?

_____

_____

_____

_____

_____

(For the authors' views, see page 85.)

S E C T I O N V

MAINTAINING GOOD MENTAL HEALTH

Nothing worthwhile is easy. However, once you become more mentally fit, it is important to *maintain* what you have accomplished.

This section of the book will give you some ideas on how to maintain improvements that you have made in your emotional fitness.

TEN STEPS FOR MAINTAINING MENTAL FITNESS

1. **Become aware of your needs.** The first step is to accept yourself. Remember, the unconscious part of your brain really knows you. When you force yourself to act differently, it will show. If your life is unduly boring—or if you feel put upon or neglected—admit it and do something about it, rather than just saying, ''This is the pits.''

2. **Let your needs be known.** Assert yourself and clearly present your feelings without attacking others. This will avoid allowing negative feelings to build up and get expressed in some negative way either internally (stress) or externally (inappropriate behavior).

3. **Demonstrate behavior that reflects high self-esteem.** This can be accomplished via body language and attitude. If you look alert and interested, and follow with a cheerful smile, others will recognize the good feelings you have about yourself.

4. **Work to improve yourself by:**

   Learning   – by reading, enrolling in academic or self-improvement classes, or working with others.

   Challenges – every few months do something new that seems interesting or fun.

   Physical   – improve your nutrition; get adequate rest; engage in regular
   health and exercise.
   appearance

   Spirit   – spend time with optimistic people; follow a spiritual program; work on projecting a positive attitude.

5. **Stop negative value judgments about yourself and others.** Become aware of how much energy goes into ''judging'' others versus finding ''unique strengths'' in others to admire and relate to.

6. **Allow and plan for successes.** Emphasize what you do well. Build on the strengths you have, and value that part of you. Remember that all successful people have regular failures but do not allow themselves to be defeated by them.

TEN STEPS (continued)

7. **Think positively.** Think about your good qualities. Give yourself credit. Keep a "What I Like About Myself" journal.

8. **Learn to escape when appropriate.** It is good to meet problems head on, but occasional side-stepping may be desirable. People often set unrealistically high standards and become frustrated when they are not achieved. Learn to add variety to your life by planning some interesting (not especially expensive) activities. Don't wait for someone else to make your life interesting.

9. **Find ways to help others.** Refocus your attention on the needs of others. Identify ways you can give to others (i.e., volunteering for a community project, getting involved in a church program, finding a person in need of companionship, etc.). Above all, show interest in others during normal conversations.

10. **Be willing to seek help when required.** When you have problems, find people with whom you can share them. If problems seem overwhelming, it is appropriate to seek professional help. Professional help is particularly indicated if the intensity of the feelings does not go away after sharing them with friends or family, or if feelings of worthlessness or low self-esteem persist.

> Ultimately, maintaining your self-confidence is the ingredient required to plan for the future.
>
> Taking *action* is the key.

STARTS AND STOPS
IN BUILDING SELF-CONFIDENCE

Confidence is not automatic. It does not come because we wish to have it. It comes because we experience success. Self-confidence must be built and nurtured.

All of us experience failures. These, to a degree, can tend to destroy our confidence. If we dwell on our failures and forget our past successes, it is possible to develop a fear of the future. This, in turn, will inhibit the rebuilding of our self-confidence.

Another way to destroy self-confidence is to always compare ourselves to others. There is always someone more capable in an area than we are (even our areas of strength). A tendency to constantly make comparisons can unintentionally lead to a decrease in self-confidence.

Being governed totally by the need to gain the approval of others will also make achieving self-confidence difficult. Finding our own uniqueness, and then building on it, is a key ingredient to ensure a good level of self-confidence.

Below is a list of "starts" and "stops" that can help you build self-confidence. Check those you feel need increased personal attention.

I plan to:

☐   1.   Start liking myself

☐   2.   Stop running myself down

☐   3.   Stop comparing myself to others

☐   4.   Start making full use of my abilities

☐   5.   Start viewing mistakes as a way to learn

☐   6.   Start remembering past successes

☐   7.   Start becoming an "expert" at my present job

☐   8.   Start finding areas in my life in which I can make positive changes

☐   9.   Start initiating a self-improvement program

☐   10.   Start *taking* action rather than just *planning* to take action.

PROBLEM SOLVING IS AN IMPORTANT SKILL WHEN DEALING WITH INTERPERSONAL CONFLICT. BEING AN OPEN PERSON, RATHER THAN STORING RESENTMENTS, HELPS.

ON THE OPPOSITE PAGE ARE SEVERAL SUGGESTIONS FOR DEALING WITH INTERPERSONAL PROBLEMS IN AN OPEN MANNER.

CONFLICT RESOLUTION

STEPS TO ACHIEVE OPENNESS WHEN THERE IS CONFLICT

The following steps will help you learn to be more open in order to improve your relationships with others.

INTENT — Openness with others must come from a genuine desire to improve the relationship rather than to win arguments. When you care about another person, openness will increase the likelihood of your being taken seriously, even when you disagree.

MUTUALITY — It is helpful to try for a shared understanding of your relationship. You need to know how the other person perceives your behavior, as well as how to communicate your understanding of her or his behavior.

RISK TAKING — Any effort at openness involves a degree of risk. You need to anticipate a potential loss of some self-esteem. There is always the possibility of being rejected or hurt by another. On the other hand, your willingness to risk depends on the importance you place on the relationship. The important thing is that you are willing to risk letting the other person react naturally when working through interpersonal problems.

NONCOERCION — Although discussion between you and another may become emotional, it should not become a tool to get the other person to change her or his behavior. Rather, the discussion should be about clarifying the situation. The purpose should be to determine what can be learned from the discussion that will help to build a more satisfying relationship. Behavioral changes should be determined independently by each person rather than each feeling "forced" by another.

TIMING — Discussion should occur as close to the problem as possible so the other person will know exactly what is being discussed. Bringing up previous situations can be viewed as holding onto "old hurts" and maintaining them simply to strike back rather than to resolve problems. Although the above is possible when dealing with conflict situations, there may be times when a "cooling off" period is necessary because the feelings are too intense for reasonable discussion.

REDUCED LEVELS OF STRESS AND IMPROVED MENTAL FITNESS ARE THE REWARDS OF THIS PROGRAM

CASE STUDY #4

GOOD WORK!

CASE STUDY #4
CAROL LOOKS AHEAD

Carol has solved many problems dealing with stress in her life. She has worked hard to understand herself and the way she relates to others. She has been honest about both her strengths and her weaknesses. When required, she has not been reluctant to seek help from her friends. On one occasion, she sought professional help when she encountered a particularly difficult situation. Open to growth and change, Carol also feels the need of an action plan to maintain the gains she has made in the past.

Carol is very busy in her roles as mother, wife and employee. Despite the demands of home and career, she does not want to get locked into a mechanical or rigid approach to life. She feels the need for a way to manage her time more effectively and to avoid becoming overwhelmed with the demands placed on her. She feels the need for emotional support from others to cope with her busy schedule.

What ideas do you have about how Carol can develop a support system to help her in the years ahead?

_____

_____

_____

_____

_____

(See authors' discussion on page 85.)

Congratulations. You have completed all of the exercises in good fashion. Before completing this program, however, it might be a good idea to take one more look at your new attitudes.

REVIEW

In reviewing this *Managing Stress for Mental Fitness Program*, it is useful to review the main points that have been made.

#1 Understand that stress and stressful situations are all around us. Each individual has an optimum stress level that acts as motivation to accomplish goals. Unrelieved stress, however, has physical and mental effects that can be difficult to fix.

#2 Manage stress by learning your individual optimum level of stress. It is important to have both physical and mental outlets for stress, including a regular exercise program, a support group of friends and/or co-workers, and adequate rest and nutrition.

#3 Most people need help to understand themselves and others. Finding ways to make contacts meaningful and productive, rather than negative and destructive, is an essential aspect of achieving and maintaining mental fitness.

#4 Learn to develop the principles of good mental health. For this to happen, you must recognize, understand and express your emotions. People with problems communicating often need extra help with this.

#5 It is important to maintain mental fitness. Work to improve yourself by learning, keep a positive attitude, challenge yourself and take care of your health. Value your uniqueness and build up your self-confidence.

Taking action to improve your mental health requires considerable determination. This book has outlined some of the rules. If it has been beneficial, we would encourage you to review the book often as you explore further.

The following pages provide some ideas about personal goal setting that you may wish to try.

GOAL SETTING IS THE KEY TO MAINTAINING POSITIVE MENTAL HEALTH.

Few people establish long-range goals. A study at a major university showed that of students 20 years after graduation, only 3 percent had established clear life goals, 10 percent had done some work in goal setting, but an amazing 87 percent had never seriously worked to establish long-term personal goals.

A person's goals should relate to his or her personal life, professional life, family life and community.

If you elect to establish personal goals, make sure they are yours-and not those that others choose for you.

Life is more meaningful when you take responsibility for yourself.

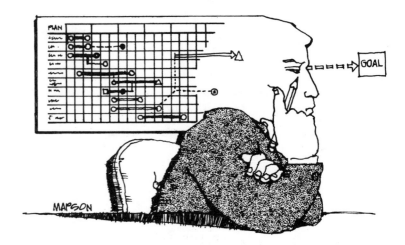

PERSONAL GOAL SETTING

Goals are significant because they provide direction for our lives. It is interesting to note that once goals have been established, they tend to be met.

For a majority of people, time is spent "meandering" through life rather than focusing on those things they really want to achieve. Thoughtful goal setting can help us determine and separate out those things that are *important* as opposed to things that are simply fun or time fillers.

Personal goals should relate to both the long term (life goals) as well as the immediate future (next week).

A.   Criteria for personal goals can be outlined as follows:

Are they CONCEIVABLE? (Can I visualize them being achieved?)

Are they BELIEVABLE? (Do they make sense or are they "off the wall"?)

Are they ACHIEVABLE? (Is it realistic to assume that I can accomplish this goal?)

Are they MEASURABLE? (Would I know if I accomplished the goal?)

B.   Goals are not appropriate when they are:

• Harmful to others

• Injurious to self

• Owned or dictated by others.

C. In order to be meaningful, goals should reach into areas where a person's potential may not be fully realized. Targets should be areas beyond ordinary achievement.

On the following pages are opportunities for you to establish some personal goals. These should be reviewed and revised on a regular basis. It is a good idea to use a pencil for this exercise.

PERSONAL GOALS

Following are objectives for various aspects of my life: ·

Family
Goals: | NEXT WEEK / MONTH | _____

_____

_____

| NEXT YEAR | _____

_____

_____

| IN FIVE YEARS | _____

_____

_____

Career
Goals: | NEXT WEEK / MONTH | _____

_____

_____

| NEXT YEAR | _____

_____

_____

| IN FIVE YEARS | _____

_____

_____

Physical
Health
Goals: | NEXT WEEK / MONTH | _____

_____

_____

| NEXT YEAR | _____

_____

_____

| IN FIVE YEARS | _____

_____

_____

Relationship
Goals: | NEXT WEEK / MONTH | _____

_____

_____

| NEXT YEAR | _____

_____

_____

| IN FIVE YEARS | _____

_____

_____

PERSONAL GOALS (continued)

Community
and Civic
Goals:

| NEXT WEEK / MONTH | _____

_____

_____

| NEXT YEAR | _____

_____

_____

| IN FIVE YEARS | _____

_____

_____

Other
Goals:

| NEXT WEEK / MONTH | _____

_____

_____

| NEXT YEAR | _____

_____

_____

| IN FIVE YEARS | _____

_____

_____

GOALS REVIEW

Now that you have completed the Personal Goals activity, make a copy of pages 78-80 and file it away in a safe place. Then on a special day (your birthday, New Year's Day, a special anniversary, etc.) remove it from your file, find a quiet place and review what you wrote.

A day or two later, re-read *Managing Stress for Mental Fitness* and revise your Personal Goals in light of your current situation. Compare your new goals with those you previously wrote, and note positive changes and areas where improvement is still needed (or desired).

If you make a habit of regularly reviewing your goals (i.e., once each year), you will be in a better position to keep your life directed toward the accomplishments *you* want to achieve. This will help you maintain good mental health because it gives you a written record of your achievements and aspirations.

TEST YOURSELF

Satisfaction is usually present when progress is evaluated. Life allows for many opportunities to check ourselves for improvement. This progress is often referred to as "growth." Good mental health is achieved through continual growth and maturation.

The assessment on the facing page will help you measure your progress in understanding mental health and becoming mentally fit.

READING REVIEW SELF-TEST

Test yourself by answering (T-true, F-false) after each statement. Answers will be found on the next page.

1. Not everyone recognizes the same circumstances as stressful. _____

2. Type B personalities are people with intense drive. _____

3. Type A personalities are more successful than Type B personalities. _____

4. A denial of our feelings when we are under stress is common. _____

5. Stress can have a direct physical effect on us. _____

6. Burnout is the logical conclusion of stress over a long period of time. _____

7. We should work to eliminate all of our stress. _____

8. Balancing one's lifestyle to include play and diet control is simply a fad and not to be taken seriously. _____

9. The expression of feelings is usually a positive step toward mental health. _____

10. Patterns of how we relate to others can be changed easily. _____

11. Conflicts should always be avoided to maintain good mental health. _____

12. Finding somebody to be like is the best way to learn mental health. _____

13. A mentally healthy person should be expected to deal with all aspects of life competently. _____

14. The need to be appreciated is something we will outgrow. _____

15. Accepting myself may be the most important thing I can do in order for others to accept me. _____

16. Mental fitness is the ability to "cope" with the joys and sorrows of life. _____

17. The ability to accept emotional support from others is a sign of mental health. _____

18. Asserting oneself is a sign of a positive self-image. _____

19. Being "open" with another person is useful if you want to improve your relationship. _____

20. Goal setting is an important aspect in achieving mental fitness. _____

ANSWERS TO SELF-TEST

1. True   (see page 4)
2. False   (see page 8)
3. False   (see page 10)
4. True   (see page 11)
5. True   (see page 12)
6. True   (see page 19)
7. False   (see page 21)
8. False   (see page 27)
9. True   (see page 30)
10. False   (see page 37)
11. False   (see page 39)
12. False   (see page 40)
13. False   (see page 43)
14. False   (see page 47)
15. True   (see page 48)
16. True   (see page 55)
17. True   (see page 57)
18. True   (see page 67)
19. True   (see page 71)
20. True   (see page 76)

AUTHORS' SUGGESTED ANSWERS TO CASES

Case #1

Maria needs considerable emotional support in order to cope with her present situation. It is also important for her to realize that she needs some time for herself without feeling guilty. The burdens of motherhood can become so stressful that she may become susceptible to anxiety and physical illness unless she changes the pattern. The more Maria talks openly about her situation and the more stress "safety valves" she discovers, the better.

Case #2

John's problems are long-standing, and one cannot assume that his basic way of relating to others will change easily. The fact that John wants help in dealing with his interpersonal problems is promising. Going to his boss, wife and friends to seek feedback about his behavior pattern is a first step. Seeking outside professional help may also be useful in helping him understand some of the underlying causes of his combative way of relating.

Case #3

Roger's withdrawal is an indication of his inability to cope with the pressures he feels. Because his behavior has changed, it is also a cause for concern. By not talking to anyone about his feelings, he adds to his potential for more severe stress. Helping Roger talk openly about his worries and fears of the future is vital.

Case #4

Having a life plan does not necessarily mean that spontaneity is lost. Rather, a plan makes it possible to direct and influence one's future rather than simply to react to the current events of life. Seeking support systems through social involvement and/or civic activities, or individual or group counseling can put Carol in touch with others who are succeeding in their own search. Knowing there will be "ups" and "downs" is important to not becoming discouraged.

NOTES

NOTES

NOTES

NOTES

NOTES

NOTES

NOTES

NOTES

NOW AVAILABLE FROM CRISP PUBLICATIONS

Books • Videos • CD Roms • Computer-Based Training Products

Subject Areas Include:

Management

Human Resources

Communication Skills

Personal Development

Marketing/Sales

Organizational Development

Customer Service/Quality

Computer Skills

Small Business and Entrepreneurship

Adult Literacy and Learning

Life Planning and Retirement

CRISP WORLDWIDE DISTRIBUTION

English language books are distributed worldwide. Major international distributors include:

ASIA/PACIFIC

Australia/New Zealand: In Learning, PO Box 1051 Springwood QLD, Brisbane, Australia 4127
Telephone: 7-3841-1061, Facsimile: 7-3841-1580   ATTN: Messrs. Gordon

Singapore: Graham Brash (Pvt) Ltd. 32, Gul Drive, Singapore 2262
Telphone: 65-861-1336, Facsimile: 65-861-4815   ATTN: Mr. Campbell

CANADA

Reid Publishing, Ltd., Box 69559-109 Thomas Street, Oakville, Ontario Canada L6J 7R4.
Telephone: (905) 842-4428, Facsimile: (905) 842-9327   ATTN: Mr. Reid

Trade Book Stores: Raincoast Books, 8680 Cambie Street, Vancouver, British Columbia, Canada V6P 6M9.
Telephone: (604) 323–7100, Facsimile: 604-323-2600   ATTN: Ms. Laidley

EUROPEAN UNION

England: Flex Training, Ltd. 9-15 Hitchin Street, Baldock, Hertfordshire, SG7 6A, England
Telephone: 1-462-896000, Facsimile: 1-462-892417   ATTN: Mr. Willetts

INDIA

Multi-Media HRD, Pvt., Ltd., National House, Tulloch Road, Appolo Bunder, Bombay, India 400-039
Telephone: 91-22-204-2281, Facsimile: 91-22-283-6478   ATTN: Messrs. Aggarwal

MIDDLE EAST

United Arab Emirates: Al-Mutanabbi Bookshop, PO Box 71946, Abu Dhabi
Telephone: 971-2-321-519, Facsimile: 971-2-317-706   ATTN: Mr. Salabbai

SOUTH AMERICA

Mexico: Grupo Editorial Iberoamerica, Serapio Rendon #125, Col. San Rafael, 06470 Mexico, D.F.
Telephone: 525-705-0585, Facsimile: 525-535-2009   ATTN: Señor Grepe

SOUTH AFRICA

Alternative Books, Unit A3 Sanlam Micro Industrial Park, Hammer Avenue STRYDOM Park, Randburg, 2194 South Africa
Telephone: 2711 792 7730, Facsimile: 2711 792 7787   ATTN: Mr. de Haas